Affirmations
Promoting
Self-Care & Self-Love

Traci J. Hinds

authorHOUSE

AuthorHouse™
1663 Liberty Drive
Bloomington, IN 47403
www.authorhouse.com
Phone: 833-262-8899

Published by AuthorHouse 01/22/2021

ISBN: 978-1-6655-1228-2 (sc)
ISBN: 978-1-6655-1229-9 (hc)
ISBN: 978-1-6655-1232-9 (e)

DEDICATION

To women everywhere; to life experiences; to self-love; to self-care; and personal growth.

CONTENTS

1. Self-Love 1

2. I Am Enough 3

3. Love Has Found You 5

4. Love Will Find You 7

5. Single 9

6. Home 11

7. Boundaries 13

8. Self-Love 15

9. Non-Negotiables 17

10. Time To Walk Away 19

11. Believe In Yourself 21

12. Forgive Yourself 23

13. You Are Fabulous.................................25

14. Fearless Love 27

15. Self-Love.......................................29

16. Success...31

17. Sleep...33

18. It's OK 35

19. Authentic Self.................................37

20. Who Are You 39

21. Authenticity...................................41

22. Self-Love.......................................43

23. Feel Better 45

24. Spa Day 47

25. Forgive Yourself...............................49

26. Matching Underwear.........................51

27. Self 53

28. Beautiful Flowers 55

29. Self-Love.......................................57

30. Exercise...59

31. Look In The Mirror.......................61

32. Forgive Yourself.............................63

33. Manage Finances...........................65

34. You Are Beautiful 67

35. Make Goals.....................................69

36. Self-Love...71

37. Mediate...73

38. Save Yourself..................................75

39. Strong Mind 77

40. Be Happy 79

ACKNOWLEDGEMENTS

Thank you to those who always encourage me to keep writing and keep creating. Thank you to my dear friends and family who love and support me unconditionally.

INTRODUCTION

Self-love and self-care are important to a healthy life. What is it and how do you administer self-love and self-care?

Self-love and self-care are much more than giving oneself a slew of expensive material things. It's really about knowing yourself, being honest with yourself, and taking care of yourself from head to toe inside and out. Being concerned about your physical and mental health and being prepared to make sure you are at your personal best or working towards your best. Self-love and self-care are about making sure your internal foundation is strong. Starting with a solid foundation and healthy self-esteem allows room to work on personal growth, healing, and affirming. The heart, mind, body, and soul need to be solid with good morals and principles, from there you build on the foundation continuously. I put these affirmations together in a specific order, an order that I believe helps get you to the next affirmation and then the next and the next and ultimately growing and knowing yourself better, and loving every moment. These affirmations helped me build through the death of my mother, dissolved marriage, parenting, work-life balance, unhealthy relationships, dating, and a slew of other life experiences. These forty affirmations reminded me to continuously work on my foundation, love myself, care for myself and keep my self-esteem at an optimal level. They have taught me I am worthy, deserve what I desire, and will be treated with respect. In sharing these affirmations with you, my hope is you'll start your day with an affirmation and it will get you through, and help you build positively on your foundation and continuously love and care for yourself.

SUGGESTED SUPPLIES

+ Bubble bath.

+ Cell phone camera.

+ Fresh flowers.

+ Good smelling soap.

+ Groupon massage coupon.

+ Pretty matching underwear.

+ Sheets, with high thread count.

+ Tea lights.

1

Self-love is the most important love.

It shall not be compromised and must be continuously developed and maintained.

The beginning of self-love is accepting and loving you just as you are.

Don't allow anyone in your space to spew negativity about or against you in an attempt to compromise your self-love or self-esteem.

Today take as many selfies as you can.

Don't stop until you have the perfect selfie.

Save that perfect selfie so you can remember how wonderful you are.

2

Before you leave your house today say these words and believe them.

I am enough just the way I am.

Any changes I make will strengthen my foundation making me a better person. Any changes I make will be for me and no one else.

I am enough just the way I am!

3

If love has found you and you are in love fantastic for you!

While in that love your job is to make you the best you, you can be.

Just keep growing!

4

Don't look for love.

Love will find you.

Be ready for love.

While you wait your job is to make you the best you, you can be.

Keep growing!

5

Single is not a disease, condition, or punishment.

It just is.

You're a catch and will get caught when the time is right.

In the meantime, enjoy life to the fullest.

Do what you love and love what you do.

If you do not know what that is try new things and discover something new about yourself.

6

Your home should be your castle, your sanctuary, your happy place, and a place where you are the queen.

Queens need a clean and clutter-free environment. Straighten up and keep it that way. Do a little every day.

You deserve and need a nice clean space decorated to your liking for your Queendom activities!

7

Set boundaries in every aspect of your life.

Boundaries keep other people's mess where it belongs with them and away from you.

8

Self-love is the most important love.

It shall not be compromised and must be continuously developed and maintained.

The beginning of self-love is accepting and loving you just as you are.

Don't allow anyone in your space to spew negativity about or against you in an attempt to compromise your self-love or self-esteem.

Take yourself to lunch or dinner. Yes, you all by yourself. Take you on a date. See what you learn about yourself.

Go ahead you can do it.

9

Know your non-negotiables. Make a list memorize them. Do not compromise your non-negotiables.

You may need to adjust your non-negotiables as you live and learn. That's ok as long as you do not compromise who you are.

Be honest with yourself and with others.

10

Know when it's time to walk away.

Don't waste too much time giving so much of yourself with nothing in return.

Pour in equally, match the energy.

Master this skill in all of your relationships.

11

Today believe in yourself!

Know that you can do anything you put your mind to.

Speak what you want into existence.

Put the work in, hold yourself accountable, and by all means pray.

12

Make a conscious effort to truly forgive yourself.

You are human. Humans are flawed and make mistakes.

Acknowledge your mistakes and learn from them.

Most importantly learn not to repeat your mistakes.

You'll need more than one day to get this one right

13

I am fabulous.

I am fabulous.

I am fabulous.

I am fabulous.

Say it over and over until you believe it.

YOU ARE FABULOUS!

14

If you love someone be fearless in that love.

Don't allow anyone to determine how you administer your love.

Love is individual and universal. Each of us love differently. Feel free to love on your terms as big and bold as you feel.

After all who wants to live life thinking, "woulda, coulda, shoulda".

Just remember always hold on to your dignity.

15

Self-love is the most important love.

It shall not be compromised and must be continuously developed and maintained.

The beginning of self-love is accepting and loving you just as you are.

Don't allow anyone in your space to spew negativity about or against you in an attempt to compromise your self-love or self-esteem.

Take inventory of who you are. If you do not like what's in stock remove and replace it with what you like.

16

The only thing holding you back from success is you.

Don't allow negativity to infiltrate your headspace. You will succeed. There will be set backs, learn from them put the effort in and press forward. Try until you've nailed it, and you will nail it.

As my momma use to say,

"Nothing beats a try but a failure"

17

Tonight, make sure you get eight hours of sleep.

Take time to leave all your worries aside.

Go to bed by 9:00 pm and just sleep.

I know, you can't sleep.

No worries. I suffer from insomnia myself.

Just lay there don't sleep but by all means, keep your eyes closed and just be still.

18

Not every day will be a good day.

That's OK.

This is when that selfie I told you to take on day one will come in handy.

Take a look at how lovely you are.

Now carry on. Tomorrow will be better!

19

Be inspired to be your authentic self.

A cliché, so you say… If you don't know your authentic self then perhaps.

It's time, no matter your age to figure you out.

First step, please thyself. Pour time into you No, is a complete sentence.

20

Who are you authentically? Are you simply pleasing others and sacrificing yourself?

Please don't.

Peel away the layers and see you! Be your authentic self. Be unapologetic about who you are.

By no means mistake this affirmation for permission to be rude or disrespectful. This affirmation is meant to lift you up so you can lift your fellow human.

21

Absolutely

Unapologetically

True

Human

Enthusiastic

Never

Terminating

In

Causes

Intended

To

Yield

AUTHENTICITY

22

Self-love is the most important love.

It shall not be compromised and must be continuously developed and maintained.

The beginning of self-love is accepting and loving you just as you are.

Don't allow anyone in your space to spew negativity about or against you in an attempt to compromise your self-love or self-esteem.

Love on yourself purposefully.

Fall in love with yourself over and over again.

23

Sometimes you are sad and don't know why.

That's ok you are not alone.

Try taking a walk, pump up the heart rate with movement.

Get a good night sleep tonight and begin to make sleeping well a habit.

You'll feel better.

24

Get a massage today. If that is impossible go to your bathroom make sure the tub is clean. Get several tea-light candles to surround the tub with them and light them.

Put more tea lights on the bathroom counter. Make sure you have pretty smelling soap that makes bubbles.

Run the bath water to the preferred temperature. Get in the tub relax and breathe.

Today clear your mind.

25

Make a conscious effort to forgive yourself. You are human! Humans are flawed and make mistakes.

Acknowledge your mistakes, and learn from your mistakes.

Most importantly learn not to repeat your mistakes.

You'll need more than two days to get this one right

26

Sometimes the simplest thing can make you feel like a million bucks.

For the next seven days make sure your underwear match and are pretty every day.

You are worth beautiful pretty things.

Your foundation is so important.

27

Spend some time with your self today.

Be good to you today, especially good.

NO negative thoughts about you, not today.

Right now, is a good time to snap a selfie.

28

On the way home pick up a bouquet of beautiful fresh flowers.

It does not have to be an expensive bouquet but a bouquet nonetheless.

Sit them on display where you will see them as you enter and exit your home.

The flowers are a reminder of your beauty and how special you are.

29

Self-love is the most important love.

It shall not be compromised and must be continuously developed and maintained.

The beginning of self-love is accepting and loving you just as you are.

Don't allow anyone in your space to spew negativity about or against you in an attempt to compromise your self-love or self-esteem.

Are you ready for your second date? Go to the movies by yourself.

Learn to enjoy your own company. If you don't you can't expect anyone else to.

30

We tend to think of exercise as punishment and correlate exercise with a diet.

Exercise is your access to the fountain of youth and a healthy mind.

Today treat yourself better get exercise. Start to exercise regularly. Start out slow and build.

You will thank yourself.

Trust and believe.

EXERCISE BENEFITS

- Improve metal health & mood
- Helps keep your thinking, learning & judgement skills sharp
- Can make you feel happier
- Increase energy levels
- Helps with relaxation & sleep quality
- Reduces pain & aids in stronger muscles & bones
- Better & healthier skin
- Aids to a better sex life

31

Take a good look in the mirror. Make sure you like what you see.

You will have yourself for the rest of your life.

You are beautiful.

Take a selfie and prove it to yourself.

32

Make a conscious effort to forgive yourself.

You are human.

Humans are flawed and make mistakes.

Acknowledge your mistakes, and learn from them.

Most importantly learn not to repeat your mistakes.

You'll need more than three days to get this right.

33

Get your finances in order.

How you manage your finances tells a story.

Poor financial management begets frustration, lack of opportunity, or more expensive opportunities by way of higher interest rates.

Save for retirement. Purchase life insurance.

Live within your means.

34

Smile.

Today I want you to smile, just smile.

Snap lots of selfies on this day of smiles and smiling.

You are beautiful!

35

Make goals, short term, and long term.

Adjust and add to the goals throughout the year and throughout your life.

The idea is to never stop challenging yourself.

Never stop moving forward and growing.

36

Self-love is the most important love.

It shall not be compromised and must be continuously developed and maintained.

The beginning of self-love is accepting and loving you just as you are.

Don't allow anyone in your space to spew negativity about or against you in an attempt to compromise your self-love or self-esteem.

Are you ready for your third date? Go do something you love by yourself.

Don't wait for others to do what interests you. Venture out solo you'll be surprised how much fun you'll have with you.

37

Take an extra-long shower today.

Not too hot it's not good for your skin. It's very drying.

Pray, meditate, sing, or whatever it is that brings you peace as the water washes away the unwanted.

38

No one is coming to save you and tell you it's ok to choose you.

Save yourself!

Don't let life pass you by waiting to be saved.

Whatever you need, you have in you.

Choose you and save yourself!

39

Your mind must be stronger than your emotions.

Teach your mind to remain in control of your emotions. Let your mind and brain be your guide.

Keep your emotions out of major decisions. Save your emotions for when they are truly needed.

40

Give yourself permission to be happy.

Then choose happiness.

EPILOGUE

A special message for those women still looking for love.

A dear friend shared this nugget with me it resonated in my soul.

You, my dear, are the beautiful flower.

The gardener takes care, nurtures, and waters the flower, in turn the flower shines.

The flower does not go after the gardener. The gardener comes to the flower.

Be smart in your movement, you beautiful flower!

Self-love is the most important love.

It shall not be compromised and must be

continuously developed and maintained.

PERSONAL NOTES

Printed in the United States
By Bookmasters